Anachronic Sensibility

Dr. Ridhima Aira Behl

BookLeaf Publishing

India | USA | UK

10
Unidades

anachronic
sensibility
aira

Presentation by *BookLeaf Publishing*

Web: www.bookleafpub.com

E-mail: info@bookleafpub.com

ISBN: 9789363312159

First edition 2024

To my parents, my dog, my siblings, and my friends

The best support system anyone could ever ask for

You're all my inspiration and motivation to keep going

Thank You

PREFACE

'Poetry doesn't cure grief, but it understands.'
- Patricia Smith

Our story has been lived out in the exact footsteps
By someone else already, somewhere else
So that is why we write and we sing and we paint
For it to be found after a moment or a hundred years in time
The legacy that becomes a lesson in another lifetime
A stranger becomes your saviour in an intervention so divine
You'll look past the skies and beyond the horizon
To see the same alignment of sentient, holy signs

Index

SICK METRONOME

Click, click, let's replay this broken spiel

I used to cry in my pillow
No lights, head down, Grey's Words playing
Flash forward and I've been screaming
Louder, louder, I scream ferociously
So messed up in my head, breaking
Self-important poetry, she says
All the trust of a poor man reaping
Call me out on a rainy day
Screw this manic pretentious damsel play
All that glimmers is so, so, so cold,
Drunken foster care of a cranberry rose
On and off, heart beating in sick metronome
Break off, break up, break me
Call off, call her, call glee
Invite my ghost to this pity party
Pacer on our dim sky, long drive story
I'll give you more reasons to hate me
Burn this effigy of a blue baby
1,2,3.. gather 'round and sip your teas
Your jasmines, your oolongs, your chamomiles
Let's dish on what a devil I can be.

RHYTHM

Bound for life by a bond unchosen
My first best friend, I'll be the best of your
lovers
Therein the depth of this connection
I founded my abandonment embassy
The deepest of my regrets are laced
With the burdens of never showing up
And for that, I am so sorry
It wasn't fair for you
And it wasn't fair for me
The complexities of our domestic
Set us up to be distant, sometimes sympathetic
The situation untangled so thoroughly for us
We grew through our teens, brawling
In lonely fallings, seldom empathetic
Hard wrestled days of making sure you're okay
I am grateful for those but if only you took a
moment
To see what they took away
Tell me did I ever refer you to my ceaseless
tear-jerker
To 'Wonder' about the dimmed twinkling of a
maternal glow
To implore for a moment of embrace, lent faith
to suffice, just enough

It's all in the past and it's all recovered
We take trips back to the war but always
convalesce
Staying through the approved sanctuary
Of rhythms affirmed, people trusted, and mates
beloved
I would still read you 'Peter Pan' whenever,
wherever
My last best friend, this will be your truest
forever.

MEMORY FIELD

The final act of all romantics is to plead goodbye
So I did, to let go, in an untimely fashion
To rest in agony, beneath an abandoned quarry
They dug a grave, and we made it deeper
After all, how much more is there to feel?
Bone dry empathy cremated in a chartered vault
I should sue these bystanders for indifference
Since my spirit has turned callous, in between
Scars filmed, in silent greys on a battlefield
Like pride bestowed upon by six strings
Steps on a corpse so devoid of sorority
A morgue created from despondent worship
Failed revival of lost and latent dreams
Pleading audits for partisan convictions
Such fickle devotion, such sour adoration
The cruelty of our jagged memory field

Tranquility of our shade, disrupted by blinding
lights
Leading us to prophetic paths till the breach
How vicious, to be lured in by stars
professing to be destiny
Fate spilled alongside our humdrum,
dormant dreams
Manipulating the quiet to keep an even score

Folding relics through cryptic metaphors
I trace so reluctantly, the evidence that bleeds
Buried deep within, outlines of a twin gaze
Only ours to have been, once condemned,
Who's going to mourn this anyway?
Now I do lie with the weeds, teary-eyed
Under starry skies, wailing, I sort through
Pleas in vain to their light's honour
Deafening, the answers that never made
An aching beauty of a life never lived
Could've been forever, one lasting lie
It never came, instead the farewell echoes
The cruelty of an undone memory field

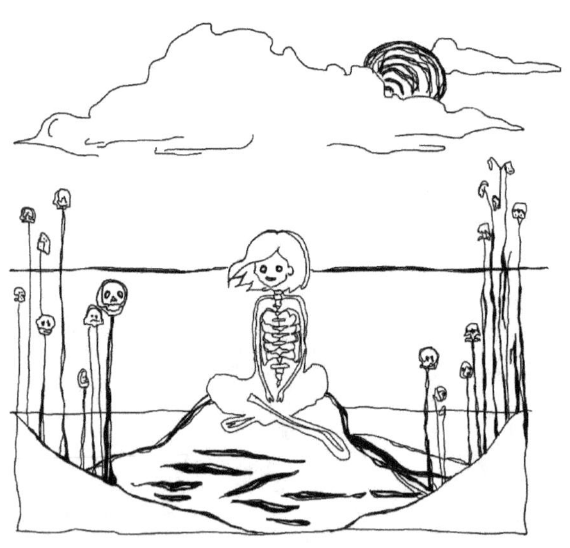

FICKLE SORORITY

And so I hypothesize, another righteous reason
To make sense of why Amelia, Audrey or Sadie
Ever crossed paths with mine,
The right place, the right time,
Three wrong best friends, our cherished vines
It wasn't me, it wasn't them, it was us, with our
Mutual frowns of fortune, 'bad influences,' they
felt
It fits now, this conferred sensibility, granted by
Trespassers on my land of hidden treasures
To awaken a run-of-the-mill aesthete, then
Mould a heart that's maternal to my childhood
self
Thank you, for bringing her around
Sentimental moments of standing on shared
ground
I am what I am because you've met me
Leave each other with an aftertaste, remember
The bad heaps more than any kin affinities
Friends break hearts just as lovers do, only better

We'd trade so much to do this in a different light
We're afraid of the peeks granted,
At sombre discretions,
Access to positive devastation

We've already felt the calm,
The mitigation of conceded courtesy,
Adjusted dispositions
In the future, we'll be careful, that time around
We wouldn't dare to be known by the other
We'd rest in peace with confirmations
of being forgotten, for good, by one another

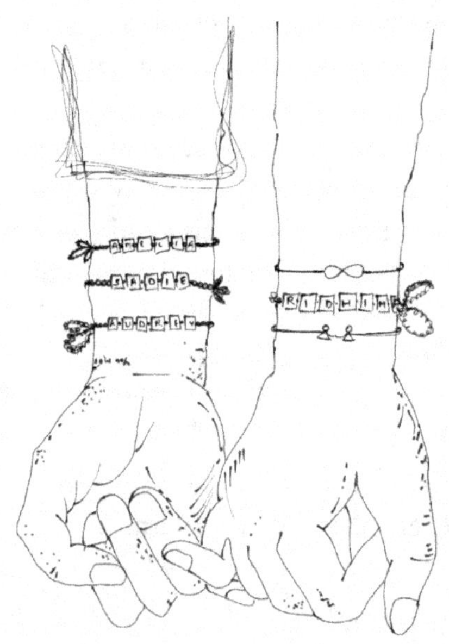

LAKE PYKARA

Lake islands marked in the shape of you
I've masked another metaphor disguised as a
lover
The same old tired underscore of renaissance
This place has never felt emptier
The address of someone who never even lived
here
Believing used to feel like bleeding
With you, however, I was back at the temple
They told her on her deathbed
That she could've been saved and they knew
how
So silly of me to only see it now
I wanted to win the game of love
I wanted it more than anyone

I don't wish to carry the weight of people
Who've left me for better, collusive collisions
Haven't I told you before, I like the ones who
stay
I don't care if that's not the way the world
rotates
I am lost, no longer my own best friend
Give me back the ones I found for myself
I had to bleed to learn the worth of rare blood

And during it all, I forgot to pay attention
To all the voices that made up the noises
Unguarded, my destiny might have leaked away
Faith and hope weren't all that they said
Taught to count my setbacks, I erased time
I couldn't face the tears of catastrophic decline

Quit the rat race once it wasn't as advertised
No, I didn't fall for the consolation prize
I want to come around in a way I can control
I want to be seen as sane by the ones who think
I'm not
I learnt it the hard way, holding on too tight
Means slowly you'll be left holding onto nothing
But I am not sure if the lesson to take away
Was to care less or to never do it in the first
place
Attachment did turn out to be the root of all
suffering
I found a little bit of healing in leasing it to
others
Learning to let the pieces fit how they please
I'm coming around to tell you I want to keep
living
I want to go back to her, she is going back to the
cliff
She is going to try to end it all again and I'll be
the one to stop it

I don't have a lot to show her yet, except this
book
Full of the comets that came at our world
Out of the blue, snatching the ones I wasn't
equipped to keep
I have been shedding pain to become bereaved
I don't know stability too well, I've heard
Of its enlightening appearances at daybreak
I am so tired of the repetitive horseplay
I fell for the princess scheme of manufactured
love
Got stuck in an emotional lunar cycle
And weeks of self-work, self-reflection
Got me only a couple of days of warm sun
I realise I'm both, the elements of my rock
And the elements of my sea
I've endorsed the waiting game for acceptance
Of dysfunctional attributes of familial
experience

And so I am back at Lake Pykara
Spilling it raw on pages ripening with existence
I've come to know love exists just here
Blooming in creations, but not their creators
My story has been lived out in exact footsteps
By someone else already, somewhere else
So that is why I write and I sing and I paint
For it to be found after a moment or a hundred
years in time

The legacy that becomes a lesson in another
lifetime
A stranger becomes my saviour in an
intervention so divine
I'll look past the skies and beyond the horizon
To see the same alignment of sentient, holy signs

REYNISFJARA

She proceeds with malicious intentions to do to
time what time did to her, just like the cold, deep
blue Atlantic waters at Reynisfjara
Where the tide curled and reeled her in, under
the surface, water filled up her lungs
Never taught to swim, mortified, she gives in to
an urge that dare not speak its name
Silenced, her screams would remain muffled for
years to come
Deceptive calm of the surface in sight, invisible
the pain she won't question
Sometimes she wondered if her life was made of
borrowed breaths
The story should have ended then and maybe
that's why the malady, on repeat echoed
Or maybe the shallow attempts to stay afloat left
her inexplicably insane, irreparably broken

The last of the sweetness of a bullied season,
spellbound to reminisce submerged treasons
Living in the spotlight of nostalgia's heed,
threatening shakedowns to remain yearning
Suspended in time at four feet tall, lending her
nightly terrors for a decade on the verge

Requiem dreams of unrequited love, what
should've been dead lingered on
Frozen their ghosts gibed how she won't ever
belong, countless indiscretions committed to
avoid being alone
Binged enough fiction to dilute the reality of her
home, she was in love with this place but the
place left her isolated to rot
Till whatever it was that the fight was about,
went away, she hid behind locked doors to feel
safe and sound

Melancholic harp strings made the back score;
should have been delicate, the times were
obnoxious
Lurking in the shadows in an allotted haven,
fearsome their 'love,' braided her fevers
Exhaustive screenings before loaning any
dough, none done of these shelters traumatizing
children
Renaissance murals of calamities on the walls;
all that prime of floral youth, tossed out to be
forgotten
She refused to pray for so long, she needed
proof of His conviction, He could've been the
only one to set her up
For a world drained of sympathy, overfilling her
cup with empathy, an imbalance bringing her to
her knees again, scraping the barrel for apathy

There's only so many times one can glue back
on, glass hearts He shatters for the world to
move along

Lonely conditions of a troubled domestic pushed
her deep into the sounds of music
Raised a hopeless romantic refusing to fade,
even as the last of her resilience snapped
Drums beating to her weakening grip on earth,
she dipped her feet in a pool of blood
Then chanted away with her Frankenstein heart,
holding the door open for everyone to depart
Outlandish was her strange rearing, standing so
tall with the lessons rooted in chords
Choreographed her memories to sync
seamlessly, she remembers the chronology of
their love leaving
So when you rethink the past, don't blame her
for all that she did, blame the damned beat
instead

Locked herself away again, she went back to the
ivory tower, searching for the lost incandescent
throne
It was getting old how nothing ever did,
preserved in time to relive the tormented
farewell set in stone

She mapped out the blocks of her hometown,
chance encounters with phantom angels and
demons
Stuck people in positions for a decade, maybe
more; and made them objects of the affection
she never got
Tides turned but not when she willed, laid to rest
ashes on the shore of the ghosts that couldn't
commit
She felt hopelessness peering through the
window, lost in translation, her futile attempts to
be understood,
The most they made of these words was only
through all of what they experienced

The scariest of feelings, the most threatening of
them all, was crooked nostalgia pouring over her
chest a longing eternal
Drowning in pitch-black hollows of recall, she
hated craving for men and women long gone,
unwillingly transported to mid-fall
Once an enthusiast of emotional immersions, she
dreaded introspections to find the pieces still
missing
Magnificent, enticing monsters beat up her
foolish angels, mangled any orators who
attempted evasion

The clues of these vacancies became apparent
once she discovered, buried under a keepsake
lock
Diary entries tracing back to when she was just
eleven, when people relatable were unseen,
unheard of
They forgot to check in if she was growing up
unfazed, spinning visceral mayhem, her mind
grew in the trenches unattended

A girl wrapped in red scarf, borrowing
void-borne affection of maternal influence
Used to go by a different name, she kept finding
reasons to undo her existence
Crushed by the weight of rouge waves
submerging a budding zest to live, homesick for
a feeling of arrival
Sprouting within, a soldier with inked cannons
awakens to take control of this haphazard fate
A force drowned her in a sea of red, then
changed the monochrome to aquamarine spreads
The views of which you'll find revered in this
tale, waiting to be read by you
Once done, she's hoping it will no longer be
hers, the pain would leave and this life..
renewed.

ALTERED UNTETHERED

Pray so intensely
on hand-tied threads
of destined schemes
reconsiderations, unforeseen
I think I might
break down
breaking you apart
because my hands
can't fight
their learned urge
to keep you warm
You dive and strive
by the ocean rocks
of crooked oblivion
bliss of ignorance
I called on you
so ceremoniously
no diamonds recovered
futile inspections
offal uncovered in
purged reunions
Sicilian handshakes
my unwavering reliance
unholy immersion
of buckwheat intentions

Dust trapped seams
washed up by a dull meer
of Ionian coastlines
chosen over mine
Who's to say
if all along
I had the tendencies
to be deranged
or if it was you
with biting propensities
to make it inflate
Adulterated inhibition
overseas darlings
future someones
to throw abandoned
We quickly went from
falling quick in disbelief
to succumbing at rock bottom
Once nowhere to be found
now stands tall ahead
the peak of surreal desolation
looks over my frustration
Fuelling temptations
to make you bleed
over and over, incessantly
Shallow waters could
then recede to Holland
once they mirror my ordeal

onto your foul reflection

My friends announced
this happens all around
hopeless fools falling
off this precipice
believing in make-believe
Snaps of shoved realities
reverberate with weeping woes
Jump off the cliff, free
tied strings, inevitably split
In dungeons, I rest
wishing on storms
theft of serenity
tormented inflictions
Where vengeance captures
treachery tainted moments
seeping through strands
of veils over stolen youth
Conscience altered
gospels repurposed
it's me before civility
Abomination committed
Albania's precluded
unfazed avenues
I loathe all of you.

POINT NEMO;

Have you been to Point Nemo, the bedevilled
ivory tower
filled with eerie noises of thumping graves,
embossed with
haunting echoes of magnetic sins, proposals of
self-sabotage

It holds you captive, the credence of a state
unscathed, isolated
An exile of ruins, convincing you yours is the
worst
Here, the universe conspires, puts up
circumstantial evidence
To make it feel like fate, kaleidoscopes of
fainted faith
Opiates dissolved in severed ties and endeavours
abandoned
Hypnotizing you in inexplicable, temptuous
ways

Fatal errors committed in emergent surgery,
Childhood scars stitching a jilted, splitting heart
Pills and blades recovered in a bedside discovery
What a grave misunderstanding of the leading
path

Gently, let me off the hook, this was repair
attempted in the dark
Any signs noticed, and then forwarded on to you
Please erase any images of me clinging to this
facade

Remove any bridges that aid you to this nemesis,
Expedite the reconciliation with your crooked
past
Someplace and somewhere, unknown to us now,
We'll cross the finish line, we'll rest in our
chosen arms
Live through the tidal waves, live through this
passage
Exist in your soul, in your mended bones, leave
the spire
Stay for this sprint, and for another broken heart;

CAPTCHA

This is my second, gallant, audacious dare
To be exactly who I am, and nothing more,
nothing less
Human tendencies expressed in anatomical
remarks
My evidence of skin and bones, and tainted
blood within

There are moments I want to check my mind
into hospice,
For a moment of peace, away from the word
jumble distorting
Into poignant melodies, revelations of
conversations
With suitors beloved, bandits detached and allies
aligned

Ailing, self-critiqued myself through their eyes
Edges so polished, they lost their grip
Every hand slipped through my overt disguise
Shimmering blood oozing from pinpricks of
a noxious past
Golden legacy overwriting ink acquired on a
sinking raft

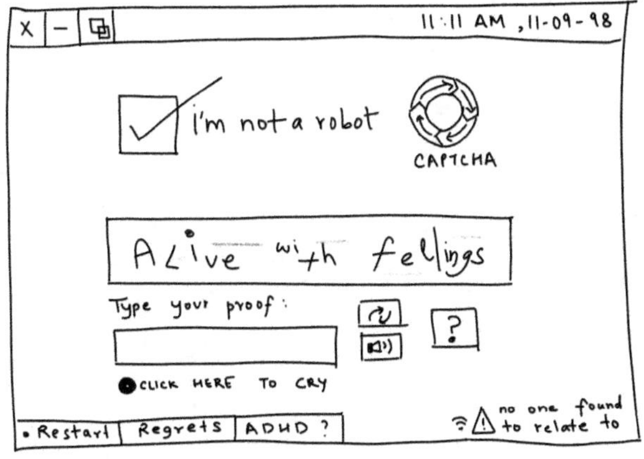

X − ⊡
11:11 AM ,11-09-98
i'm not a robot
CAPTCHA
ALive with fellings
Type your proof:
?
CLICK HERE TO CRY
Restart | Regrets | ADHD ?
no one found to relate to

I grew up to disprove the prophecy, transfigured
into a renegade, hiding in plain sight
Is this enough proof, that I'm alive?

Alert caution to the sign in the stars
Only look back for a moment
Any more than that, any longing stares
The devil will latch onto you and take you for a
ride afar
And along you will encounter, engage and duel
every sinister feeling
you have ever refused to feel
In quicksand, stranded, paralyzed, you will be
asked to kneel.

BUCK BUNNY

I have never found the brakes on my pen's
reckless ink
I confessed incessantly till we reached the moon
I professed my insanity on the dark side of the
eclipse
Stuck with it as if you were ever going to
resuscitate
Finally, I left by myself to cry my way to Saturn
Oh, what a muse for life, what a tragedy to beat,
marvellous
Skin screeching from the flashes of all our days
The innocent, the mistaken, the vengeance
Did your sister acquit you of this bewitched tale
You asked me at the rift of a splitting thrill
'Did this mess you up?' Well, what if it did?
How do you plan to fix it? Or even face it?
This was holy blood spilled for free
Your crime was sacrilegious
You maimed all my Gods in the sky
This was your pride playing Odin
My faith abandoned somewhere in the dump of
your trysts

It's embarrassing how much I could still give in
to you

C SCH
Honeysuckle
ch : 8 : A game
of chance

Just to pay back for every medicinal recall
from when we were both just four feet tall
I never told you this, but they were carefully
woven beads
Of purity unseen, I used them like drugs during
your time away
I used them to numb the grey of my thriving
decade

My heaven-sent ghost, hauntingly saving me
through an ill-fated epoch
What a stupid thing to have believed, ghosts
only come back from love that perishes
Still, I wanted so sincerely to be buried next to
you, in a beautiful cemetery
Holding onto all the love and my cherished
bunny.
I end this story, so tragically unfolded, nothing
like the one I saw on that silver screen.
I'll take your goodbye leave with this note on
your red-letter grave.

And now that you're no longer the one, I will go
look for another story to love.

RETREAT

When the going gets tough, I retreat into my
silent corner
I plan and plot like I would split your world into
two
Afraid of the worst that could come from a
frenzied confrontation
I write, in my cowardice, and then the words
strike the page
Like we were standing just a feet apart, like I
were throwing black ink in your face

I wouldn't know to describe the journey from
pen to paper
It's as if the ghost of some poet long gone, takes
possession
And sees my catastrophe as an object of their
affection
From the first verse till the very end, we join
hands
To disguise this misery like a blue heart's
coefficient
As if the whole thing wasn't calamitous, just an
indolent repetition
Of verses prewritten, stories forgotten in this
unfathomable prospectus

of human existence.

Cynically, I give up the good fight
In the eye of the tornado, I try and decipher the
intentions of this uncanny playwright
And there, hiding in my sympathetic notes of
euphonic correspondence with a deity
I figure I have been so tight-lipped, my fears
turned to tears and they filled an ocean in me
It wasn't the abandonment, it wasn't the
infidelity, it wasn't the duplicity
My silence, a slow venom, it corrupted me and it
chased me
Into a bottomless pit of reclusive exodus
An ocean of words, of feelings never uttered, of
forgotten vulnerability
An ocean of endorsed fear, not the adversity, the
ocean of solitude killed me.

d.p.s

hot-headed debacles and my cooling systems
failing
judgemental scorekeepers of favours extended
flummoxed approaches to sensitive questions
embarrassing confessions on Facebook
messenger

bittersweet memories of lunchbox days
scars for life braided through bottle green ties
the mellifluous call bell of class dismissal
water cooler talks of flame-ignited scandals
such a tortured time in summation
yearbook indentation of 'lord, never again!'

morning prayers of trying to be an optimist
the whole class list united with a clenched fist
almanac notes of mischief captured
BlackBerry messaging of getaway
transgressions
collecting scholar badges like compensation
for hours missed at the play station
annoyed with the reps for denying us our
birthright
roars of disruption echoing through the corridors

DELHI   PUBLIC   SCHOOL

bittersweet memories of friends for life
bus stop rides and splash fights
chalkboard names and library stairs
smell of lent books and wai-wai indulgence
the bullies and the pets, bickering away
8th graders doing their best impressions

such whimsical moments of a stress-free time
little did I know, without this,
I'd never have anything that I call mine

there's an offer up for all my wealth
to replace this desk job for that beloved wooden
desk
pencil mark running through the centre
'I'm right and you're left'
a dozen years of pure insanity, a beautiful time
in retrospect

APATHY BEQUEST

Thudded, paced, drops of a teardrop waterfall
Flows through the passage of unwavering times
An heirloom indifference of mutual disdain
budding
from resonant satires of failing to persist
Forever willing to reset, opposing sporadic
burials
Of conversations unhinged, the ones we insist
The scale of the disruption resonates with the
Suffering done, to be left unattended in disbelief
Ripped images of carefully embroidered
bonafides
Views of a once-serene valley, now reek of riots
Resembling the views of a hometown window
Behind locked doors of instilled shame and
perpetual submissive obedience
The daring act of a dainty existence, bearing
more
Weight than nature must have intended
Ridiculous to be this dense, we never speak
The audacity of possessed intellect, how dare
she
Perform all roles for a one-act play, then takes
notes

Of disappointment from an audience
over-engaged
The beauty doesn't choose but settles for the
beast
Stopped dead in the tracks before any butch
barricades
Mothers of these indolent creatures curb their
dreams
No wonder the patriarchy piles up to the neck
The chokehold of forgotten debts after all
Rests within the cult of matron ancestry

STRAY

Look at me now
I remember to forget
And I've forgotten to forgive
Neither was as promised
There was never any bliss
I don't overthink it now
I just do it anyway
Whichever comes to me first
Kill or ameliorate
My latest trades are all chance
The stories so fictitious
No patience to untie any knots
Tangled loops in cheap gold necklace
Hurled decisions on the board
Hate you's, Love you's, all across
I passed my life through a filter
I never fixed the dial on the sieve
What remains is now free of me
My smearing brushes, my cleaning fee
I don't know why I kept you
I don't know why you're gone
Stray past the reasons to feel
Reverse psychologies and frozen texts
Cynical motives, and us moving on.

DOPAMINE HUSH, AN ORCA LEGACY

Here goes the mystery of my whale tattoo

Orca is an unfinished punchline
Interrupting my plans, calling the bluff
Bending the universe so I'll have more luck
Where the proof of words isn't enough
There your ataractic glances are
I dream of them when I dream of love
A love not lost, but a love that allows
Deep dives into the ocean that is my heart
Apex predators of unchallenged destiny
Mysteriously cathartic, your greetings
Gentle beings of the giant blue
You make the loud beat stop
In the most peaceful way
Unlike any temporary rush
Enchanting me with
Your dopamine hush
Guiding me back home
Whether that abode
Be a place or a feeling
The movement of your tail
Turning grief into power
Counting on my dream catcher

To catch you for more of your ecstasy
Singing through the sound of rain
Leading me to arrive reformed
Just in time, as soon as my time's up
My chosen patronus, my chosen protection
Riding waves to the edge of the world
Then bringing me back to where I belong
Showing me to reclaim lost and treasured gold
Engraving new meaning onto artefacts old
Taking it all back, what was always
And will always, be mine first

CYNOPHILE

'You are the memory that won't ever lapse
When twenty-five years have suddenly passed
Wherever you take me, it's clear I will go
Your love's the one love that I need to know'

My wildflower, my 11:11 wish
You are my prayers answered
A saving grace that came in
Through the cold that precious November
Radiant within the ranks of angels
Blessed my world with your company
Greeting me in sacred January
Inscrutable your boundless affection
Came to me wrapped in red and ever since
I've basked in the warmth of your embrace
Every ordinary moment holds
Extraordinary beauty with you
Whether the weather be good,
Whether the weather be bad,
Or even when it's good enough,
Every moment spent with you, shines
I could never find anywhere in this age
My best man, my loyal guard
You know it somehow, when I'm sad
So sweetly you rest your head on my lap

Your paw prints imprinted on my skin
You're the guiding light in my starry sky
You cure my dysania and lead me to light
You rescue me from demons within
Smiling and laughing at me
With your blush pink tongue
Golden luminosity of your silhouette
Peaking through the daylight
A hummingbird filling my skies
With profound melodies
Of gratitude, of respect so full of life
Lifting me up to be safe and sound
Pouring faith into my depleted cup
Always acting like the damsel in distress
Distracting me from complications of the herd
Tolerating my neediness stemming
From famines of impoverished states
I pour over you all the love I once craved
To you, I confess all my sins
And share with you all my secrets
All of this anointed bliss,
Comprising mostly of you
You are the correction drawn
Over the fault in my stars
Boop at me with that perfect nose
Digging holes in the yard as I scream 'Nooo!'
Your symphonic cries asking for attention
Anxious whimpers so impatiently
Calling on the delayed chicken

Growling when I try to steal your bone
Chasing you in circles round and round
Around the dining table
Intense sounds of your rapid panting
Forever and always in my earshot
Sniffing your way through everything
I know you'd protect me from any monsters
Even though you're startled
At the sound of a pen click
Chasing the litter sprinting through the park
Best friends with a hose pipe
That you love to rip apart
Watching me dance at odd hours of the night
Judging my moves in tiresome sighs
Stealing my side of the bed
Every time that I get up to wee
I've got a million pictures of you
But I don't think it's nearly enough
I imagine maternal glow to be
Made of a similar essence
With you, I am never living in the past
I'm scared of the time that's ticking
I want to pause the moment
Hold on to you in this light
For you, I'd endure that fateful goodbye
For what you lend me are a thousand moments
Of pure love, a gift I would never know how to
return
I already know I'll find my way back to you

We'll be playing ball till the end of time
We'll do it all again, somewhere in the blue
skies
Your love is inexplicable
I could spend my whole life trying
To put it into words,
But I know I'll fail to define
What this gift of pure joy, happiness
And at times sadness too, means to me

It's a shortcoming
I never wish to overcome.

'You are all this heart of mine
And there you will remain.'

ALEXITHYMIA

54

I beg you to speak no more
I want us to change this track
Whoever thought becoming undone
Would be such a drag
The neighbours peek through
Who'll make it past the wall?
Offending in defense of my solitude
What's missing? Stolen sighs,
Or a willingness to bleed pools?
No, I am not going back
To the rooms of medicinal cities
It was time done, undeserved
A castaway outcast, underserved
Went down fighting for just one
Recognition of familiar souls

The narrative is devoid of candour
I feel so powerless, so destitute
Watching the people I've loved
Grow into people I don't
Scrolling through my top five
With feet touching shallow waters
Fleeting desperation to get picked
Straight out of those Okayama gardens
Woven hushed into exulansis

Don't you bother to relate to me
I've witnessed the people I honoured
Shrink into people I won't

They once all fit in a box
Like pieces manufactured oddly
To make up a blue, tempered soul
Now their print has faded
Revealing such conditional amour
Leaving a vault laden with tombs
Distress aligns with foreign, laboured sensations
Of mourning colored souls with a heartbeat
Psychotic woes of imagined reality
Plagiarized from a thousand silver screens
This metaphor will never be absolute
Cornered pages will split from her alexithymia
They won't ever know how the feeling wounds

SYMPHONY

57

Grant me one wish, and one wish alone
I would ask for a background score
Of all occurrences, fleeting and lasting
You're the olive branch extended
By an upturned destiny, emending
Give me evidence of existence
When they try to patronize me
No matter how dense the haze
I am always apparent to you
However deep the well
My hands in perpetuity, reach for you

I have my doubts over faith, over
Deities that cash in rewards for strain
But I believe in you, religiously
You have never stopped my heart
Eternally point me to Polaris's starlight
Cleaning up after sanguineous wars
The void of synths is my kryptonite
Playlists like acquired fingerprints
Of life lived through folds of seasons
Bestowing permission to belong
In exile, on occasions when I don't

All that I've felt could only be contained

In the strongest of relics available to misuse
I keep maps of moments lived, buried
In the depths of your symphony
Pure concoctions leading to my eternal salvation
The magic of music is of transtemporal
epiphanies
The strongest love I have ever felt
It's supernatural sorcery at its best
Within you, you hold diary entries
Of nostalgic yearnings, clandestine interludes
Of distress signals, wailing stray innocence
And entwined fabrications of deluded fantasies

Glaring cautiously at turning tables
Melodies woven through the good old days
They could someplace, somewhere
Be souvenirs of notes that sing pain
Once when I lost myself, I lost
The silhouette of your eloquence too
It was the loneliest I had ever been
The most detached from my spirit
Separated from my intentions
And convictions in a dynamic labyrinth
It was limbo, it was purgatory
It was death ringing my doorbell

I found my way back crawling
& have carved many a trail since
To trace my way back to your shade

For uncalculated wrinkles in time
That could deafen my world again
I burned my whole life down
Revised dedications to those notes
Drank from the luminous elixir
Transfigured my harmonies
Into associations indestructible
Engulfed in the flames of a phoenix
As many times, as time needed
Changed beats of resuscitated senses
Sounding a lot like unclaimed legacy
Coming back stronger than ever before
The dawn of a new age comes forth

LOVE BITES

cheating on blue with purple

I got a little red mixed with my blue
so now my pen only bleeds this lavender hue
voluptuous shadows
tease dance around my lips
luring us into this risqué abyss
it's breaching into my fantasy pool
the lights are down low
seems this mist wasn't seasonal
turns out to be a perennial glow
and now the red's burned to a maroon
so this hue is now more of a purple
matching the marks by the scruff
that go ravaging all over down below
this anticipation has changed my brain's
chemistry
can't leave this on hints anymore
now the sugar's loaded on high
for a while now, I'll be only looking at the sky

BRITTLE BURBERRY

Perspectives earned over bridges burned
Time elapsed, what once stood the test
Has now collapsed to ruins urged
Lost control of the words slipping past
The tip of your tongue, unchecked
Oblivious, which one could bring in the last
straw
Reminiscent of all the times before
Where disrespect got swept under the rug

I won't condone the terms of your apathetic
Fadeout branching off a narcissistic delude
In my mind, I knew then,
Drew borders you shouldn't have crossed again
That's the cost of living it your way,
It all unravels in the blink of an eye
Dominoes set in motion till the silence
reinstates,
Someone else could be living their way

Brittle Burberry shakes the till to its core,
Somebody's blood and another's tears
Traded like fool's gold for inexplicable hosing,
Years without end of oblique narrative
Appearances can be deceptive more than once

You feel the thorns if the rose gets close enough
Olive branches become poisonous too
When used like tokens to strike again

Candied candour could be concealing
Elements of indelicate surplus
Life is a clickbait story
Traps of pretence luring you to glory
Feminism is a dirty word
In towns ruled by money's worth
We're wary of damsels in distress
Feigning deprivation with insincerity

Harbouring axes to grind
Nicking the safe once the unrest unwinds
I can see you staring my way, blank faces and
Furious eyes, flaunting borrowed audacity
A contention of your bread lies,
Glaring so acutely with hypocrisy
Bearing the consequence of impudence
Boundaries between us with no ends

ANACHRONIC SENSIBILITY

What is this growing up to be?
Why are there so many feelings to feel?
I could jump into the olden days
Any moment now, for all future time
Any liquid to put to sleep, this mental row
Memories cramming into each other
The stench of stall floors and me shedding
Tears of lost and stolen innocence
Now published into defenceless public records
Judged in masses where I never belonged

Mercurial distribution of allies and foes
Material pleasures to distract from meaning
Leaving things behind, over and again
Growing up has ceased to become mundane
I don't belong in the valley of desperation
With beautiful people delaying their expiration
I don't want to be wary of everyone looking my
way
They measure every word as if I painted it
In crimson-coloured tinctures, on my face

Sinister setting of unfaithful Romeos
Collecting wary-eyed, steadfast Juliets

Befuddled perception of a fickle love
Enduring immortality until conjugal indentation
It's forever and always, spilling over
With promises of 'til death do us part'
The dagger of flipped predilections
And the mortality of a stupid heart

The idiocracy committed by this lover's
advocate
She tried to submit into evidence, eye-contacts
Alongside glances of slaughtered faith, conduits
Of what would later be unclaimed and
relinquished,
Construed as a petitioner deranged
Not your mutiny, not your infidelity
My affection was deemed counterproductive

Searching for the next steps to follow
I went to outer space for a face-off
The planets denied any engagements
They hadn't even seen the horoscopes
'Stop accusing me, peony human!' said Saturn
Mercury couldn't care less, renegading
I realised these oracles must have been
Meteorites carrying our kryptonites
We are alone here, unsynchronizing
We weren't meant to wipe this out
It's all deliberately accidental
Nothing was meant to be, it just so happened

These pages didn't turn by the wind of age
These pages were burned in a spiteful rage
Smiling at your faces like I was taught how
Forcing predilections like you always wanted it
somehow
Then, I would have been a level-headed damsel
Seeking love that wasn't doomed to perish
The lens of your perception has shifted to grey
Long letters wouldn't reek of a wench's cringe
Revered instead as fearless memos of a romantic
Once a marquise so insanely in love
In today's world, I am just insane

I'm a lightweight when it comes to forsaking
Diving into melomaniac roars as soon as I step
in
Downsizing tragedies of youth into mental
diagnoses
It's either constant connection or blocked postal
codes
What could I possibly say to nullify the creeks?
Good girls are brought up to presume it true
They believe in everything like it's still the first
day
Insolent preening by a righteous society
To craft a looney woman's fitting image
Bedazzled by the likes of dazzling insinuators
Dethroned when the lease terminates

Foolish girls do get raised this way
They believe in everyone like it's still the first
day
People here don't speak what they mean or
Mean what they speak, words here are devoid
Of any real substance, caution, they're mostly
lies
Tell me, what do wise men speak of this?

Everyone betrays you, then affords you first-aid
In moments of self-reflection
It makes them feel better because apologies
Are all that one can hope to extend
But no amount of band-aids can repair wounds
That need knives and needles
Stitching mangled skin like pretentious modern
art
Sewing patches onto faded straitjackets
True power would have lied in staying quiet
Almost as if it wasn't their business
They move onto finer days free of mushy songs
I look through their windows hoping I'm still
better off

I write sad stuff about bad things
And that was the way to process
Yours, mine, and everyone's being
Because I have been around town
And dealt with people who walk about

With heads held high, and their insta disguise
Oh! How it pisses me off
Picture perfect phoney pageant smiles
Never having processed a single thing
In their teeny, little, incomprehensible minds
I am sure of it, here I couldn't belong
The times have never been more wrong

Maybe this should have all been left unsaid
But I have learned from the best of rebels
I thrive by telling on the unnecessary
Lunacy is out loose coming to get you
Make you say profanities behind curtains
Of anonymity that fills your ever-leaking
Holy grail of standing over everything
Yet, amounting to absolutely nothing
Trying to fit in here brings in problems of peace
A fish drowning in the bluest of seas

My highest branches couldn't touch heaven
If the deepest roots hadn't crept to hell
Together they form a colossal maze
Of routes unfathomable in ancient days
Laced within are instructions to liquidate
Disfigured egoes, seats to be reclaimed, for
Being memorable enough as stunning ghosts
Blinding me strikingly in the nostalgia of it all
I am certain again of how I don't belong

Present only as a mould, the heart's always
withdrawn

Spilling the beans on twisted acts of the past
Waking up to more devastation every passing
hour
What a shame, no news here is ever bad enough
An unsaid acceptance of the atrocious lingers
Desensitized to the godawful absurdity going on
Nobody's your lover, nobody's your friend
Mistrust penetrates even blood-borne threads
They've rigged the system and poisoned our
fixes
In the age of red flags and carnal politics
I still seek friendship, still seek love above all
else
It baffles me, just how worthless will that love
be
The one we leave behind for our children
I know it to exist because I feel it in my bones
So tell me, anyone, how could I possibly
belong?
Was I misplaced in time at the stroke of a devil?
Were times another really any different?

In my heart,
I know I don't belong
I long for a home
Where my mind

Could finally
Let its guard down
And In harmony
Sing along

Someday
Fate must align
Rid me of longings
For a suitor beloved
And desires
Of lost treasures

Someday
Fate will align
So a wandering soul
Sets free the zealot
No more lost
No more vulnerable
A carefree juvenile
Could finally
Live in peace